Laura Shur

CHRISTMAS TUNES
FOR THREE

for six hands at one piano

Novello

Cat No 10 0282

CHRISTMAS TUNES FOR THREE

1. AWAY IN A MANGER

PART A: Bass

arranged by
LAURA SHUR

PART B: Middle

1. AWAY IN A MANGER

CHRISTMAS TUNES FOR THREE

1. AWAY IN A MANGER

PART C: Top -
play one octave higher

arranged by
LAURA SHUR

2. DING DONG! MERRILY ON HIGH

PART A: Bass

2. DING DONG! MERRILY ON HIGH

PART B: Middle

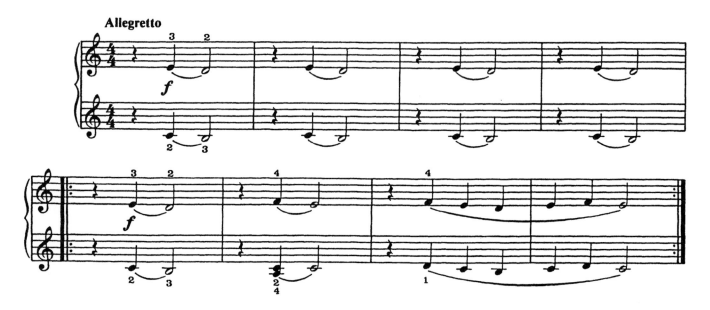

2. DING DONG! MERRILY ON HIGH

PART C: Top-play one octave higher

PART A: Bass

3. WE THREE KINGS

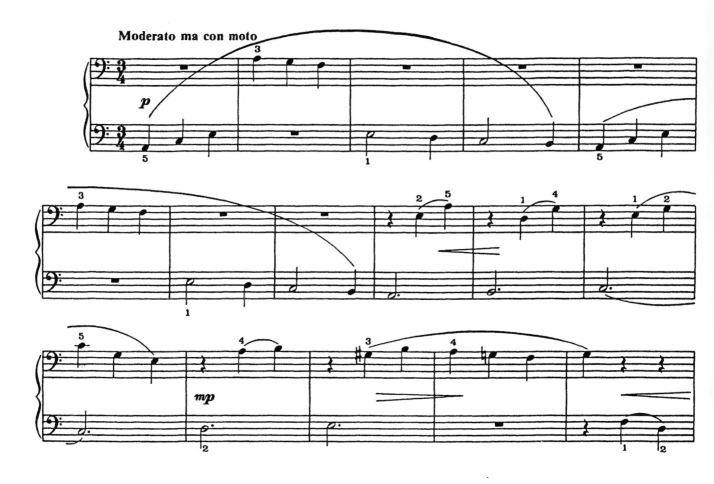

PART B: Middle

3. WE THREE KINGS

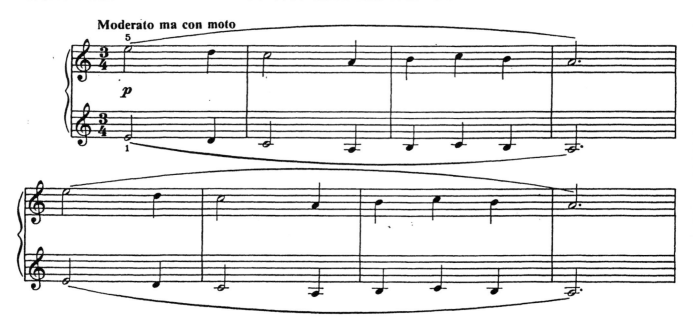

PART C: Top-play one octave higher   **3. WE THREE KINGS**

WE THREE KINGS (cont.)

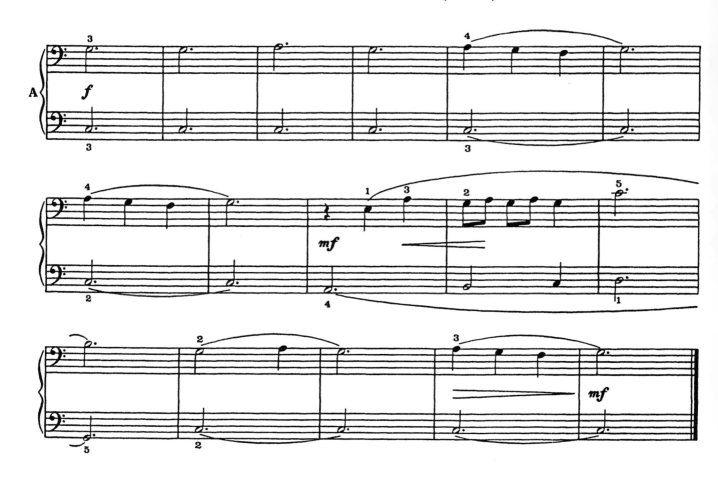

WE THREE KINGS (cont.)

WE THREE KINGS (cont.)

10

PART A: Bass

4. MASTERS IN THIS HALL

PART B: Middle

4. MASTERS IN THIS HALL

PART C: Top -
play one octave higher

4. MASTERS IN THIS HALL

PART A: Bass

5. DECK THE HALL

PART B: Middle

5. DECK THE HALL

5. DECK THE HALL

PART C: Top -
play one octave higher

6. WE WISH YOU A MERRY CHRISTMAS

PART A: Bass

6. WE WISH YOU A MERRY CHRISTMAS

PART B: Middle

6. WE WISH YOU A MERRY CHRISTMAS

PART C: Top - play one octave higher

Allegro giocoso

Published and Printed in Great Britain by
Novello and Company Limited, Borough Green, Sevenoaks, Kent.